WHAT READERS ARE SAYING:

"As parents, there's no greater success we can have in this life than raising up our children the right way. Failing to plan for our children and their future could easily unravel all the hard work and care we put into our family every day. It's been a worry of ours for years but where do we start? *"Good Parents Worry, Great Parents Plan"* is right there worrying with us. Laura Meier lovingly starts off the book with a sincere concern for her own children and then heads straight into real planning by breaking it down in a simple, direct and concise way. It's been very easy to understand and has all the information we parents need to plan for our families accordingly. We've been looking for this book for years! Thanks Laura!!"
—Christian Jacobs with Shanna Jacobs, Co-Creator of Yo Gabba Gabba, a Nick Jr. and Nickelodeon Award Winning Television Show.

"As a family physician and the father of three young children, I understand how important it is for parents to confront seemingly morbid issues such as determining medical wishes at the end-of-life. Doing so now, however, can create a great sense of security and relief knowing that you and your loved ones have had that conversation out loud and your wishes will be respected in the unfortunate event something should happen. I applaud Laura for devoting her professional life to this important work and for writing this book to raise awareness about the special issues pertaining to estate planning for parents with young children."

—Jay W. Lee, MD, MPH, FAAFP, President-Elect of California Academy of Family Physicians (CAFP)

"As a pediatrician and a parent, I cannot recommend this book more highly. An essential guide for families planning their estate written in everyday language by a mom and lawyer who knows her stuff."

—Ameer P. Mody, MD, MPH, FAAP, Assistant Professor of Pediatrics at Children's Hospital Los Angeles

"As a mother and a family physician, I share Laura Meier's vision to 'build a stronger, more intentional family and create a lasting love that can never be taken away by anyone or anything.' Each day in my office, I have discussions about life and death with my patients. Yet, I now feel inspired to establish a similar relationship with a family attorney and to discuss with my husband the family values we want to leave as a legacy to our children. In this book, Laura guides readers past the barriers of heart wrenching 'what ifs' and the overwhelming complexities of family relationships to clarify the value of estate planning with confidence, humor, and grace."

—Michelle Quiogue, MD, FAAFP, 2013 Family Physician of the Year, California Academy of Family Physicians (CAFP)

"As a pediatric anesthesiologist and mother of four children, I highly recommend this book. Written from one parent to another, this book is sure to become an essential resource and tool for any parent trying to do what's right for the benefit of their children.

—Suzanne Strom, MD, HS/Assistant Clinical Professor and Director of Residency Program, Department of Anesthesiology at University of California Irvine

"My wife and I made a New Year's resolution to 'get a will' for our children. We contacted Laura and are so thankful we did. She and her team conscientiously worked with us to help us answer all of the questions and then take the necessary steps to make sure everything is taken care of. It is so much more than just a will. I sleep better every night knowing that we have formal plans for our children, our finances, and ourselves if anything should happen. I would start the process by reading this book. The book breaks down each key topic into small, manageable pieces and also clarifies a lot of unfortunate assumptions that people have about how things would be handled. It is a great way to start thinking about your answers to these questions and take the next step—call and get it finished!"

—Jeremy Zoch, Executive Vice President and Chief Operating Officer, St. Joseph Hospital

"Laura Meier is bright, knowledgeable, and very, very insightful. Her new book hits the nail right on the head when it comes to estate planning for young families. It contains lots of important and valuable information that every young couple with children should (no, must) have."

—Jeffrey R. Matsen, Esq, *WORTH* magazine "Top 100 National Attorney," Author of *The Ladder of Success*

"Families must pass on their values before they pass on the value of what they own. Parents must give their children a spiritual and emotional inheritance before they give them a financial inheritance. Wise mothers and fathers realize that any one of us could be gone tomorrow; therefore, we need clear instructions for the guardians, trustees, fiduciaries, trust protectors, executors, and other people who will attempt to reflect parental values to the next generation in our absence. Thank God, Laura has taken the time to write a book that can help all of us. Laura is uniquely gifted to write this book because she is a technically competent attorney who understands the importance of building all legal documents around solid commitments to family and spiritual values. I will be recommending this book to my clients."

—Tim Voorhees, JD, MBA, Author of
The Best Zero Tax Planning Tools

"You can pay a lot of different professionals a lot of money to educate you on what you need to do to plan for your young children, or you can read this book. I suggest you read the book!"

—Jamie Hargrove, JD, CPA, Co-Founder and
CEO of Netlaw

"Insightful, Educational, and Motivating. *Good Parents Worry, Great Parents Plan* is a must read for any parent who wants to make sure their children will have the best in life."

—Brian M. Davis, JD, Founder and
CEO of Orange County Young Executives

"This book is the perfect combination of a lawyer's head and a mother's heart. Parents will be shocked to learn just how difficult they can make things for their loved ones if they do not have an estate plan in place, but will come away inspired and educated on the steps they need to take to protect their children."
—Laurie Rowen, JD, Co-Founder and Managing Partner at Montage Legal Group

"As parents, we spend so much time and effort on how to prepare our children for the future, yet we often overlook the reality of how to protect and secure our children's future if we're no longer around. In this book, Laura Meier reveals the critical steps parents must address to plan effectively for their children's future."
—Krishnamoorthy Narasimhan, PhD, Portfolio Manager at PIMCO and Adjunct Faculty at The Paul Merage School of Business, University of California Irvine

"Such a simplified approach without minimizing the information. Taking legalese and making it understandable. What a great resource for anyone looking to protect their family and their legacy."
—Nathan Fikse, Financial Representative at Northwestern Mutual

"Don't let what you don't know hurt your family. Laura's book successfully highlights why parents should not leave their financial security and children's well-being to chance one more day, and how they can successfully take control today."
—Andrea M. Casaw, Financial Advisor at Morgan Stanley

"As the Executive Director of Boys Town California and as a father, I know firsthand that parents and children need education, resources, and support to build a strong foundation and enjoy a bright future. Laura Meier's book will no doubt provide tremendous value to all parents seeking to create a closer and more purposeful family."
—Lawren Ramos, Executive Director of Boys Town California

"More than a set of legal documents, a good estate plan captures your vision and values of how your legacy should carry on after you are gone. For young families, this ensures that your children are cared for in a manner that you desire. For families with older children, an estate plan can ensure that the assets that you accumulated during your life can be disbursed in a manner that conveys your values to the next generation. Laura's book is a won-

derful first step and highlights how you can get the most from a comprehensive estate plan."
—Roland Ho, CSPG, Executive Director of Office of Planned Giving, University of California Irvine

"This book was simple, quick, and life-changing! It pointed out needs we didn't even know we needed to be concerned about as parents, and made us realize how important it is for us to put our wishes into place for our sons."
—Adam Kennedy with Lyndi Kennedy, former Major League Baseball second baseman, ALCS MVP 2002, World Series Champion 2002

"Hot diggety! Finally, here's a book that explains the reasons why legal planning is vital for parents in plain language! Laura's personal experience and professional commitment shine through and will help guide parents to make clear, conscious, strong decisions for their loved ones. Understanding the legal landscape you live in the moment your first child is born is an empowering step in your journey as a parent. Laura's book will help you wrap your head around the complexities of planning so you can actually get something done. What a relief it is to know that you've done everything you can for your family!"
—Martha J. Hartney, Esq., Boulder, CO

good parents worry,
great parents plan

good parents worry, great parents plan

The Guide to Protecting Your Child with a Will and Trust

LAURA K. MEIER

Printed in the United States of America
ISBN:978-1-63385-014-9

Design and Printing:
Word Association Publishers
205 Fifth Avenue
Tarentum, Pennsylvania 15084
www.wordassociation.com

This book is dedicated to my late

grandmother, Elizabeth King—the first author

in my family. Your love for writing left

me a great legacy to honor.

§

Foreword

When I created the Personal Family Lawyer® program, I did so dreaming of lawyer's like Laura Meier taking up the mantle of a whole-hearted shift in the way lawyers serve their clients. Seeing Laura step into the role of trusted advisor to her clients and bringing what I originated even further into the world with this important book is incredibly satisfying.

It first occurred to me that estate planning lawyers were missing something critical in their planning for young families when I, myself, had a young child and even though I had an estate plan in place, I recognized it didn't fully cover my daughter if anything happened to me and her dad.

And, I knew if I didn't know how to ensure my children were cared for if anything happened to me, neither did anyone else because I went to the best law school in the country and then worked at the best law firm in the country.

I was out to dinner with my husband one night when it occurred to me that if we didn't make it home, she would be taken into the care of child protective services while they tried to figure out what to do. Our wills weren't easy to find, and even if they were, everyone named lived across the country. And, it wasn't like we included phone numbers and contact information in our wills.

It dawned on me that we left the person we cared about the most in the care of a 16-year-old babysitter with no real backup plan.

Given that I was an estate planning attorney at the time, I was shocked that no one had ever taught me how to make sure my children were really taken care of if anything happened to me.

As I looked even deeper at the standard planning most estate planning attorneys engage in for families, I saw even more significant holes. My children were at risk. And yours very likely are too, but you are in the right place to get these holes fixed right away and put your mind at ease.

Laura has covered these holes and their solutions in this book, so read on if you want to make sure that if anything happens to you, your loved ones know exactly what to do, your children will never be taken out of your home and into the arms of strangers, and your family has someone to turn to for guidance, love, and care, no matter what.

—Alexis Neely, JD, Founder of *Personal Family Lawyer*®

CHAPTER ONE

Parents Make the World Go Round

You make your children's world go round.

You feed them, you provide for them, you bathe them, you take them to music class, take them to school, coach their teams, cuddle them, discipline them, pour your insights and beliefs into them, and every day you try to become a better person for them. There is nothing you would not do for them, and in fact everything you do is for them.

Even when you manage to sneak a little time to yourself, which rarely happens, they are always on your mind. And you never ever stop worrying about them. They know by now that no matter what, they can count on you. You make their world go round.

That's why it would be simply devastating if something unexpectedly happened to you or your spouse. Your child's world as they know it would end, and life would be very confusing until someone else transitioned in to take over.

For parents who have not actively planned for the "just in case something happens to me" scenario, this transition period can last years as the courts try to sort out all kinds of issues, such as who should raise the children, and who should control the money, home, and life insurance proceeds left behind.

Eventually, the courts will sort through it, and the transition period will end. Unfortunately, however, the consequences from parents not having done their estate planning can negatively impact their children for their lifetime.

This is why you are likely asking the single most important question most parents ask once they have a child: **What would happen to my kids if something happened to me?**

This book is intended to be a simple answer to that very complex question. It's everything you need to know about what type of estate planning your family must have so your child's world will always go round.

CHAPTER TWO

Learn from My Mistake

I'm an active parent like you. I have four children ages ten and under who are handfuls in different ways. My days are packed with managing their school schedules, homework, practices, and needs, and with running a very busy trust and estate planning practice. If there is a shortcut for getting something done and having it done right, then I want to know about it.

For parents like you and me, there is a good reason we put off some of the bigger tasks in life. We are just too busy trying to get through the day. When clients first walk into my office or come to one of my Kids Guardianship Workshops, they often tell me that one of the main reasons they put off their estate planning is that the whole thing just seemed so overwhelming and they didn't have the time to figure out what they really needed or who could help. They want the easy, quick, simple fix so they can finally mark estate planning off their to-do list and never have to think about it again.

I get where they are coming from. I was once in the same boat. When I became a new mom, I was already a lawyer (just not an estate planning lawyer yet). I knew I needed a will—or at least that's what I thought I needed—but I was so overwhelmed and busy caring for a new baby and learning my new role as a city attorney that I too put off my own estate planning. I really didn't have a good excuse considering the law firm I worked for had an estate planning department in it!

I knew I could walk downstairs and ask the estate planning attorneys what I might need. You'd think that would be easy enough to do, but I never seemed to have enough time to go down there to talk with them. I continued to put off my estate planning until the day before I was about to have a medical procedure done where I'd be going under. I knew I had to get something in place, so I went on the law firm server and downloaded a will and a health care power of attorney.

On the server I did notice some documents called a "living trust," but it looked pretty involved. I didn't really know how it worked and what was entailed, so I just skipped over that one. I assumed it was probably just a legal document for rich people.

I slapped my name on my will and health care power of attorney and named my parents as guardian. Ten minutes later, I grabbed a couple coworkers and had them watch me sign. Besides being a bit creeped out by the sight of my name on a will, the whole thing was very easy. I put the documents in my office drawer and never wanted to think about them again. In my mind, it was mission accomplished . . . finally! My estate planning was done.

Thank God I didn't die.

I discovered just how bad my check-the-box approach to estate planning was after I eventually decided to leave big law firm life behind and start my own law practice. I knew I wanted to work with families, so estate planning seemed like the best field for me. As I began my training through some of the top estate planning programs in the country, such as Personal Family Lawyer® and Wealth Counsel, I immediately realized that the will and health care power of attorney I had thrown together years earlier would not protect my family if I were incapacitated or died. Here's why:

1.   I didn't have a temporary plan in place to ensure that my son would be immediately placed with my family instead of going into temporary foster care until the authorities found my will and a judge appointed my parents as the guardian.

2.   I named my parents to be the guardian of my son if I died, but I never specified if I wanted one of them alone to serve if the other parent had passed away or if they had divorced. I also didn't name backup guardians in case my parents couldn't take on that

responsibility. This means that a judge, after a long court process, would have had to make this decision for me.

3. My will would not have spared my family from a long, expensive court process (known as probate) should I have died.

4. The documents I downloaded would not save my family from having my money tied up in court, which meant someone else would have to support my son until a court order was issued to allow access to the money.

5. The will I downloaded was not set up to pass my assets to my son the way I would have wanted. My only choice was that he would get all of my money outright at age eighteen, without restrictions. That would have included my life insurance.

6. I picked someone I knew to be in charge of all the financial responsibilities if I died, like selling my home and managing money left to my son, but I never really thought through if that person was the best person to handle investments, work with the guardians I chose, and serve long term in that role.

7.　　I thought all I needed was an end-of-life directive, and I didn't even know there were other steps I needed to take to make sure my family could talk to the hospital if I were incapacitated.

8.　　I never thought about leaving behind something far more valuable than money to my young son so he would always know the special love I had for him.

9.　　It never occurred to me that I didn't have a trusted family attorney who had helped me set up the plan—someone my family could immediately turn to in my family's time of need.

10.　　I never had an action plan in place that would make these documents actually work when they were needed. They just got stuffed into my desk at work.

11.　　The documents I had were outdated because I had subsequently had another child and moved since then.

Clearly, my check-the-box approach would have failed the people I love. I realized that graduating from a top law school and working at a major law firm did not exempt me from making the same terrible mistakes most parents do when they throw together an estate plan. But that was the problem all along: *I didn't really think about it.* I just wanted to check the box and be done with it.

Today, as the founding partner of a top California trust and estate planning law firm dedicated to guiding families with young children, I educate and caution parents of young children on the danger of the check-the-box approach to estate planning. I share with them what I discovered after my own trial and error:

There is no quick-and-dirty approach that leads to an estate plan that will protect your family forever. There is only a quick-and-dirty approach that leads to estate documents that will fail.

Don't think—as I had—that downloading a will or any legal documents is anywhere close to having an estate plan. Legal documents alone cannot ensure everything you do day in and day out for your family will magically continue without you. It doesn't work that way.

You may be thinking, *This isn't me. I have an estate plan and I paid a lot of money for it. My lawyer is one of the best in town and he charges $1,000 an hour.* I am sorry to disappoint you, but paying a lot of money to a top lawyer in town *still* does not ensure that you have the right plan for your family. You've just found a much more expensive way of checking the box.

I am going to educate you on what type of estate plan your family needs. And I am going to warn you that it is going to be different from traditional estate plans that your parents probably have, your rich friend has, or that you've seen online. This is because **you need an estate plan where your child is the center of the plan, and not an afterthought.** Your plan will need to have unique protections and strategies because of your children's young ages. And once you clearly understand what type of plan you need, I will show you how to go about getting the proper guidance and assistance for putting the plan together.

CHAPTER THREE

Starting Your Planning from Ground Zero

If you are like most parents with young kids, you haven't done any estate planning yet.

I love meeting with new clients. They come into my office looking like they have a confession to make. They admit to not having any estate planning, even though they know they should. I'll tell you what I tell them: (1) I'm not a priest, (2) They're still alive, so it's not the end of the world, and (3) Most parents have put it off just like they have. We're busy!

A shocking 69% of parents still haven't even legally named a permanent guardian to raise their kids if something happened to the parents. Are you one of them?

When I speak at our Kids Guardian Workshops, I always ask the crowd the same question: How many adults in California already have an estate plan? I hear rumblings in the crowd—5%, 20%, 10%, 1%, and so on. Well, you may be surprised like them to learn that **100% of adults already have an estate plan.**

Confused? Yes, that's right. You already have an estate plan. That's because, if you haven't done your estate planning for yourself, your state has already done it for you. And believe me—you're not going to like it.

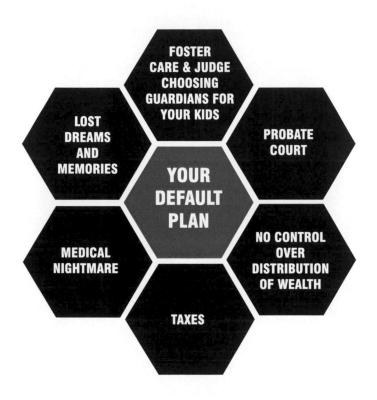

This default chart shows all of the areas of your life that will have to be dealt with if you become incapacitated or die. When you fail to make plans for these areas in your life, your state will have to step in and clean up your mess.

Your state will subject your family to years of courtrooms and lawyers, and determine everything from who should raise your kids to who should control your money, and even whether you can be kept on artificial life support if you're in a vegetative state. While there are a lot of things the state will have to do for you that you won't

. . . if you haven't done your estate planning for yourself, your state has already done it for you. And believe me, you're not going to like it.

like, there are also a lot of things they won't do for you—which is even worse—such as preserve your legacy; protect your money from lawsuits, predators, and creditors; and make sure your kids don't blow all their inheritance at eighteen.

If you want to know if the state's plan is a good one or not, just ask someone who lost a loved one and had to turn to the state to clean up their affairs. They would do anything to go back in time and have their loved one create an estate plan. It truly is a nightmare, and knowing it could have been completely avoided makes it all the worse.

The good news is that you can avoid your state's plan by setting up a proper estate plan that is designed to fully meet the needs of your young family. This will give you a lot of peace of mind and save your family a lot of time, money, and heartache.

As we look at your options for setting up your estate plan, I encourage you to start taking notes on what you need to do. Every technique I will cover will be essential to creating the best plan for your family.

How many parents do you know who could benefit from reading this book?

Call Meier Law Firm today at 949.718.0420 and request 3 copies for just $18.

CHAPTER FOUR

The Physical Care of Your Children

Your love for your kids is unconditional and everlasting. Sure, they drive you crazy now and then, and you miss your sleep and free time, but there's nothing in the world you would trade for having your kids in your life.

It's hard to even imagine that something could happen to you that would prevent you from being there for your children like you are now. That thought alone probably triggers emotions so deep inside of you that you would rather not have to go there. But, as you are well aware, you are mortal. You are reminded of this every time you turn on the news or hear about a friend of a friend or think about having lost someone close to you.

You think about how precious life is every time you kiss your little ones goodbye, take a vacation without them, or leave them with a new sitter. In the back of your mind, you think, *I hope everything is okay while we are apart.*

Unfortunately, if the unexpected does happen and you don't have your own planning in place, your state has to step in with their plan for your kid's care.

STATE LAW

If parents become incapacitated or die, their minor children can be placed in temporary foster care, and a judge will have to decide who should raise them, unless the parents have legally named <u>temporary</u> and <u>permanent</u> legal guardians for them.

I know this seems harsh and cold. You're right—it is. But it is the law.

There was a family in San Diego, California, a few years ago that had this state law apply to their family. The husband and wife were tragically killed in a car accident, leaving behind three young children. If that wasn't heart wrenching enough, what happened afterwards was devastating.

The parents unfortunately had not named temporary or permanent guardians for their kids. Because of this, their children were placed in temporary foster care for a short period and then thrown into a long and catastrophic court battle where the late mother's sisters argued over who should raise them. After a very long and sad legal battle, a judge—who had never even met the late parents—had to make the final decision on who should raise the kids.

The tragedy wasn't just the tens of thousands of dollars wasted in court, or the fact that a judge who did not even know this family had to make the call on who should raise the children. That was awful. But not as awful as three young boys, having just lost their parents, being placed in the care of strangers and then being thrown into a year-long court process that left their family completely torn apart at the time they most needed stability.

Could this happen in your family?

YES. IT COULD.

Can you stop this from happening in your family?

YES. YOU CAN.

What do you need to do to stop this?

You need create a comprehensive estate plan that addresses your children's care, not just for the long-term, but also during an emergency.

CHAPTER FIVE

Creating an Emergency Plan

If something unexpectedly happens to you, that means it was, well . . . unexpected! Most parents, and even most attorneys, don't give enough thought to what should happen during the initial emergency period after something has happened to the parents. They tend to focus only on the long term after a parent has died.

When parents come to my office for a first meeting, I ask them a simple question: What will happen today to your kids if you don't make it home from this meeting? They suddenly get the deer-in-the-headlights look and start to freak out a little. "Well, um, let's see, my ah daughter's school has an emergency contact card, so they'll call my friend Patty and she'll pick her up."

I keep asking follow-up questions. "Ok, so then let's say it's getting late in the evening and Patty still hasn't been able to get in touch with you?" That's when they realize Patty has no idea how to get in touch with relatives, and they start to throw out words like police and hospitals.

"So," they ask—and you may be wondering too, "what do the police do when they show up after getting a report that parents are missing?" They may just leave the kids in your friend's care, but if parents are missing or the police discover they are incapacitated or were killed, and there are minor kids involved, it is very likely that Child Protective Services will be notified.

Child Protective Services is a state agency that oversees the welfare of children. It usually becomes involved when parents are missing, are seriously injured, or die, and young children are left behind. It's a liability for them not to get involved once they are notified of such a situation.

The goal of Child Protective Services is to place children in safe situations, ideally in the care of their family members. However, Child Protective Services will not automatically leave your child with your babysitter or even your family member if you are missing or have died. This means that your children could temporarily be placed in temporary foster care—in the care of complete strangers—at the moment they need love and security the most.

As this chart illustrates, temporary foster care can happen during the gap between the time of your incapacity or death and the time a judge either appoints a temporary guardian, signs off on your choice for permanent guardians, or appoints a permanent guardian because you did not.

Recall the San Diego couple who was killed in a car accident and left behind three young boys. Their children were temporarily placed in foster care until a judge temporarily assigned them to an aunt's care while their family members battled in court for over a year over who should be permanent guardians.

Could your children be placed in temporary foster care before being placed with permanent guardians? Yes!

Can you keep this from happening? Yes, you can.

You do this by making sure your estate plan addresses not just what should happen in the long-term for your kids, but also what should happen during the short-term. A short-term emergency plan should include temporary care for your children, medical directives, and an alert system.

Temporary Care for Your Children

Your emergency plan needs to include legal documentation that authorizes people you trust to temporarily care for your children during an emergency, so they will not have to be placed in temporary foster care.

Temporary guardians (also known as standby guardians) can be caretakers, friends, family members, or other adults you trust who you know would provide your children much love and comfort during a crisis. We usually recommend that parents name at least four or five temporary guardians in case one or more are not available to help. Temporary guardians should live within twenty minutes so they can quickly get to the children during an emergency.

It surprises me how many estate planning attorneys do not even know about standby or temporary guardianship laws. I attribute this to the fact that most estate planning lawyers work with the old and wealthy, and thus planning for little children and avoiding temporary foster care is not something they typically encounter.

As an estate planning attorney and as a mom, I can tell you that **temporary foster care is the NUMBER ONE concern parents have when I ask them what bothers them the most about not having an estate plan.** It bothers them more than their money being tied up in court, it bothers them more than taxes, and it bothers them more than not having made their own medical wishes known. The fear of temporary foster care can be alleviated simply by naming temporary guardians.

Children's Medical Directives

An emergency plan should also include medical directives for your children so the people you want can make medical decisions for them if you cannot, and your wishes for their treatment and care can be honored.

Recently in Los Angeles, California, a husband and wife were killed in a car accident on a busy freeway. Their daughter was in the car with them and was seriously injured. She was rushed to a local hospital and immediately placed under the care of Child Protective Services. Several major medical procedures were performed on her, all at the direction of strangers who had no idea what the parents' wishes were for their daughter's treatment or care.

Don't leave it to complete strangers to make major medical decisions concerning your children. Make sure you complete medical directives for each of them.

Alert System

Completing legal forms that authorize others to temporarily care for your kids and make their medical decisions during an emergency is not enough. There needs to be an alert system in place so these decision makers can be brought in immediately.

At our firm, we notify temporary guardians in advance that they have been chosen for this role and explain to them what they need to do in the event of an emergency. We also provide them instructions and documentation they need and could present to Child Protective Services and eventually a court so it is clear that they have legal authority to keep the kids in their care.

We provide family emergency cards for parents to keep in their wallet and in their car, so if they were in an accident, the police and medical caretakers would know that they have minor children waiting for them and who to call. We even have instructions for caretakers and babysitters so they know who to call if the parents fail to return.

We recently used a new babysitter for our children, and before we left for our event I showed her our emergency instructions on the side of our refrigerator. She looked at me like I was the strangest person she had ever met. She said, "Are you not planning on coming home?"

I laughed and said, "Yes, I'm planning on coming home, it's just that I want to make sure you know who to call if something unexpected happened to us."

She said, "I have never once had anyone I've babysat for say that to me." (She wasn't impressed by it—she just really thought it was weird!)

It made me realize, though, that most parents don't have any kind of emergency plan in place for their kids beyond filling out school emergency cards. Would your children's caretakers truly know how to contact your family in an emergency, and would your family even have the legal authorization to help?

Let me encourage you to get an emergency plan in place right away. When you set up your estate planning, make sure you work with an attorney who understands the importance of having an emergency plan so you are fully addressing both the temporary and long-term needs of your little ones.

…get an emergency plan in place right away…

CHAPTER SIX

Creating a Long-Term Plan for Raising Your Kids

If something were to happen to you and your child's other parent, you'd need a designated person who can step in and continue raising your children. This person is called a permanent guardian. If you do not choose a permanent guardian yourself, a judge will have to make this decision for you.

I've heard so many times from parents that they avoided their estate planning because they and their spouse couldn't agree on who should be the permanent guardian. Even my husband and I have struggled with this decision, and we are estate planning attorneys. If it's tough for parents to decide, imagine how much harder it is for a judge who has never even met the family! It is our moral, legal, and parental responsibility to make this decision ourselves.

A permanent guardian can be a family member, friend, godparent, colleague, or someone else you know, love, and trust, who is willing to be legally responsible for raising your children.

Telling someone you want them to be a permanent guardian is not enough! E-mailing your mom to say you want her to be the guardian is not enough. Telling your spouse you would never allow the mother-in-law to be the guardian is not enough. You have to legally document your wishes.

To help parents make the best possible decision, we have them follow an easy three-step process.

Easy Three-Step Process for Choosing Permanent Guardians

This easy three-step process gets most couples 80% toward making a final decision on permanent guardians. I've found that the remaining 20% comes from working in a private setting with a trusted attorney who regularly counsels parents with young children in making this decision. Oftentimes you need that objective third person to keep the discussion on track and gently guide you based on years of practice and insights. If this sounds like therapy, it basically is. We often joke that we may be attorneys, but when it comes to estate planning we are more like therapists!

So, here is how you get the first 80% of what you need.

Step One

Take out a blank piece of paper and write down all of the potential people who love your children and could potentially serve as guardians. Potential options include grandparents, aunts and uncles, cousins, adult siblings, friends, or coworkers. Ideally, you will write down at least five to seven names. If you have a couple in mind (i.e., your brother and his wife), then write both of their names together on the list. We'll talk later in this book about the best way to name couples. For now, just write down all the names.

This is not the time to be evaluating people or shooting down names your partner suggests. All you are doing here is making a list of people who love your kids.

Step Two

Put away your list of potential people and take out a separate blank piece of paper. Write down a list of your top three qualities or characteristics you would want a person who is raising your children to have (i.e., age of guardian, religion, lifestyle, location of guardian, integrity, etc.). I like to identify these qualities as the "non-negotiables," meaning you will not compromise on these criteria.

One thing you should never consider is the financial resources of the potential guardian. As parents, it is our responsibility to leave behind the assets or life insurance necessary to raise our kids. Your potential guardians are not setting aside money just in case they might need to raise your kids. So if you want to set up your kids and potential guardians for success, then you need make sure you have the proper financial resources in place. If you don't know already what amount would be needed for your family, you need to contact your wealth advisor to find out. If you don't have an advisor, find one tomorrow. There is really no point in putting *wishes* in place. Money is essential for turning wishes into an actual *plan* for your kids.

It pains me when I hear that a young parent has died and not left a sufficient amount of money behind for his or her family. This often results in kids losing two parents because the surviving parent now has to single-handedly provide financially for the family while also being the primary caretaker. Make sure this couldn't happen to you.

Step Three

Compare the first sheet that lists your potential guardians and the second sheet that lists your priorities. Rank in order the "potential people" you listed, from first choice down to last choice, based on who offers or possesses most, if not all, of your top three priorities.

Our simple three-step process is not magic, but it does help you look at things a little more objectively. It sets the platform for your trusted advisor to work from when coaching you to a final decision.

Once you have your permanent guardians in mind, it's important that you haven't made any of the common mistakes most parents, and their attorneys, make when designating guardians.

Mistake One: Not Being Both Objective and Subjective When Picking Guardians

Think back to when you first fell in love with your spouse and decided to marry. It was probably both an emotional *and* logical decision. You knew you felt a deep love and emotional connection, but you also evaluated character, qualities, values, and what type of life you would build together.

Similarly, when it comes to choosing guardians for our kids, we should not only be thinking about who we love and their relationship with our child, but also be evaluating their qualities and values and the type of life they can actually provide for our child.

I remember talking with one couple who were at odds over guardianship. The wife wanted her parents, and the husband, who had been raised by his single mom, felt as though he would be deeply betraying his mom if he did not choose her as the permanent guardian. The husband's emotions were really affecting his decision. And even though his mom would have been a great choice, I'm not sure he or his wife believed she would be the *best* choice.

His head was deeply conflicted with his heart. He said, *I don't want her to feel like she is losing something,* mindful that she had experienced great loss in her past.

Many times our emotions and loyalty to those we love can overpower our decision making when choosing a permanent guardian. This is normal. But, keep in mind that you are not taking anything away from someone you love by choosing to make someone else a guardian. You are simply choosing to not add an additional role on top of the special role they already have in your child's life.

If you stick with the easy three step process and make sure not to let your emotions disproportionately control your decision, you will be making both an emotional and a logical decision when choosing who is best for the permanent guardianship role.

Mistake Two: Not Naming an Heir and a Spare

Notice how most royal families have an "heir" and a "spare," and that they never travel together? This is because if something happened to the first in line to the throne, they need to have a backup so the line will continue.

We may not be royals, but there is something big we can learn from the heir and spare concept when it comes to setting up guardianship. You need to make sure you have designated backup guardians just in case your first choice for guardian can't do it or declines to serve. I usually suggest couples list two backup guardians.

Mistake Three: Naming Couples without Conditions

Ideally, you would list a person or a couple and if something in their life changed or if something unexpectedly happened to them, you would just update your guardianship wishes. But this is not always feasible.

For example, what if you picked your mom and dad to serve as guardians, but your mom and you were killed in an accident together? Would you still want your dad alone, or would you rather have your sister, who was your second choice, for guardian? This needs to be made clear.

Or what if you picked your brother and sister-in-law, but they were no longer married at the time of your death? Do you still want both of them, or maybe just your brother alone, or neither at all? This needs to be made clear.

Maybe you really want your in-laws, but only if they will raise the kids in your hometown. This needs to be made clear.

Some attorneys will tell you not to name a couple at all in case one cannot serve or the couple divorced. This is easily remedied simply by making sure that when you name a couple, you also address your wishes for common circumstances, such as death or divorce, that could result in one or both of them not being able to serve.

I had a client before who, when asked about adding conditions for guardianship, said to me, "Well, I really want my friend, but can I make it a condition that she divorces her husband first?" No, but it opened up a great discussion on whether she really wants her kids to be raised in his home if she is so opposed to him being a guardian. Make sure you and your attorney talk through any unique conditions you face or requirements you have, and discuss whether you can or should legally include them when identifying a guardian.

Mistake Four: Having the Guardians Manage Your Children's Money

Sometimes the person you choose to raise your child is also the best person to manage the money you left behind for them. But this is not always the case.

Raising children and managing money are different skills. Your spouse may be the most hands-on parent in the world, but may not be the best person when it comes to making investments. Or maybe your spouse is great at making money, but not so great at arranging the children's birthday parties.

When you choose a couple to serve as guardian, hopefully between the two of them they are the best choice to raise the kids and manage the money. But what if they aren't? Or, what if you are concerned about the fact that if your guardian is managing the money, there isn't any additional outside oversight to ensure the money is being used in the best way for the children?

I like to assume the best about people and I'm sure you do too, but assigning your guardians to also manage the money is something that should not be done lightly. In many cases, it makes a lot of sense to leave the money management to a different family member or an outside professional or institution who is really good at doing just that—managing money.

Mistake Five: Not Excluding Guardians

One of the most difficult parts of my job is when I sit down with a couple to go over guardianship and discover why someone in the extended family is not being considered for guardianship. In some cases, the situation is so severe that we actually recommend that person be excluded from ever being considered as a guardian.

You may be wondering why someone you didn't pick to be the guardian could end up being appointed by a judge, even when you've already identified several other people that you would want to serve as guardian.

This happens in the rare circumstance when guardianship is contested, the guardians you wanted declined or have died, or a judge concluded it was not in your child's best interest to be placed with them. If that happens, you could end up in the same situation you were in before you named permanent guardians yourself. That is when a judge begins looking within the family to find a suitable permanent guardian for your children.

In most states, judges give preference to your parents and your spouse's parents, and would have to choose between them. If that is unsuccessful, they will start looking at your siblings or your spouse's siblings. This is why it is imperative that, in addition to naming who you want to serve as your permanent guardian, you also exclude anyone in your family that you would never want a judge to consider, should the guardians of your choice not work out.

I recall sitting in my office with a couple, where the wife broke down in tears as she painfully explained to me why her mom should never be considered as the guardian of her children. I recall a husband apathetically reference his biological dad when asked if anyone should be excluded. He said something along the lines of, "Yeah, knowing him he'd show up for once if money was somehow involved."

These are sad situations, and my heart goes out to people who have to exclude a guardian. I also admire and am inspired by people, who despite their unfair upbringing, have gone on to enjoy healthy lives and create the family they always deserved.

If someone in your family comes to mind as I talk about excluding guardians, there is a very delicate and confidential way to accomplish this. The excluded person would never find out unless the guardianship you had set up was contested and a judge had to start from scratch.

Mistake Six: Not Leaving Behind Instructions and Other Important Information

We've all heard the expression *kids don't come with an instruction manual*. All of us parents have had to learn on the job. We've had to learn through others' examples, and plenty of trial and error, how to meet our children's needs and build a world for them.

Inheriting kids, though, is different. They've already had a life before being placed with you, and they have just come through something very traumatic. Obviously, parents should do everything possible in advance to ensure a successful transition. **This is why you should have an instruction manual for raising your kids!**

At our firm we call this document "Instructions to Guardians," and it is a key way to ensure that your guardians understand your child's needs, beliefs, and support systems, and your goals for that child. Believe me—your guardians would really appreciate some kind of guidance so they can raise your kids, honor your wishes, and make sure they are meeting what you have laid out as their emotional, physical, spiritual, and intellectual needs.

One of the big areas your instructions should address is what other relationships your child has that are important to them and that you want your guardians to help foster. For example, continuing to see grandparents may be on your list. You would think this is a no-brainer, but your guardians have their own lives too, and time gets tight, so it is good for your guardians to know exactly what was important to you. You don't want to create a situation where your wishes are unclear, and suddenly relatives are turning to the court system to continue to have access to your children. Set your vision from the get-go so that before your guardians even consent to serving as guardians, they know what the expectations are.

I hope that you feel a huge step closer to naming permanent guardians for your kids. Let me encourage you to not leave your kids at risk one more day. Make a commitment with yourself and your spouse that you will make this decision right away.

Let me encourage you to not leave your kids at risk for one more day.

How would you like to name permanent guardians for your kids for free?

Visit meierevents.com to register for our Kids Guardian Workshop, or call Meier Law Firm at 949.718.0420 for details.

CHAPTER SEVEN

Passing On Your Money

If you do not have a properly set up estate plan, you are relying on other methods for passing your money on to those you love. And, as you'll discover, these other methods are all problematic and create a serious risk that your money will not go to support your spouse and children the way you intend.

Without proper planning, there are three primary ways that your assets will pass to your spouse, children, or other family members. The first two ways I will briefly discuss, and then we'll spend a lot of time looking at option three, as this is where almost everyone ends up if they don't do proper planning.

Option One: Joint Ownership

One way for you to pass your money to someone else is to just own the asset with them while you are alive, so it will automatically pass to them when you die, and vice versa.

For example, if you and your spouse are both the account holders on your checking account, the money will automatically pass to the other person when one of you dies.

Likewise, if your deed lists you both as the owners of your home, then it will automatically pass to the other person when one of you dies.

In the legal world, we describe this type of arrangement for holding assets as joint ownership. While this type of arrangement may seem ideal because everything can pass automatically, it can actually be very bad. Here's why.

When you or the other person dies, all of the money passes to the other person outright, without any restrictions or protections. This means the other person can give your share of the money away to anyone they want, such as a new girlfriend, spouse, or business partner, with no guarantee it will go to your children. It also means that if your spouse gets sued, gets divorced, or faces a lawsuit later on, the money you left behind can be taken away from him or her. Eventually the other account holder will die, and unless they did their estate planning, all of that money (or whatever is left of it) is going to end up in the hands of the court system.

Option Two: Designated Beneficiaries

Another way you can pass money to someone else is to name them as a beneficiary on an account or policy so the money automatically goes to them upon your death. If you have a life insurance policy or a retirement account, you probably remember listing a beneficiary, which is the person the money will go to when you die. If you are like most people, you probably named your spouse as the primary beneficiary and your children as your backup or contingent beneficiary (if you listed a backup at all).

Passing money this way poses all of the same problems you face when money passes through joint ownership. The money passes with no protections or restrictions, meaning your beneficiary can give the money away to whomever they want, and have it taken away by creditors, predators, lawsuits, and a new spouse. There is no guarantee the money you leave behind will ever make it to your children.

Even more problematic is when you name your child as a beneficiary. Because your child is not yet eighteen, if you died, a court would have to step in and set up all the necessary safeguards and protections a minor must have, assuming you did not do this yourself.

Lastly, your family could face a huge problem if you have not kept your beneficiary designations up-to-date. We read about this all the time—a man dies, for example, and his wife discovers that his 401(k) had an ex-wife listed as a beneficiary. Or only one child was listed as a beneficiary and the account was not updated to include subsequently born children.

There are many potential problems that may arise when naming beneficiaries of your accounts. I will show you later on how you need to designate your beneficiaries so the money will pass to them the right way.

Option Three: Probate Court

The third option for passing money to someone else, assuming it did not automatically pass to another joint account holder or adult beneficiary, is for it to pass through probate court. Probate court is a government-established process that your money (that was not held jointly or did not go directly to a named beneficiary) must pass through in order to go to someone else. Oftentimes money passed through joint ownership or beneficiary designations ends up in probate court when the second spouse dies or when money was left directly to a minor.

Before I dive into the details of probate, I want you to think about your assets for a minute. I bet there's at least one account or asset you have that you own all by yourself and thus could be subject to probate immediately upon your death, even if your spouse is alive.

I can't tell you how many times I've met with married couples, and when I pull out the deed to their home, only one of them is listed as the owner. They'll say, "Oh yeah, only my husband could qualify on the loan, so that's why I'm not on the deed." Or, "Oh yeah, my wife owned her home before we got married—that's why she's the only one on the deed."

My favorite story was when I met with an older couple who had been married fifty years, and when I looked at how they owned all their accounts, there was one with just the wife's name on it. I asked why this was, and the husband shook his head and said, "Well, that's my wife's honey pot. She said she needs it in case the marriage doesn't work out!"

Whether you have a "honey pot," a home only in your name, or any other asset that is yours, my point is that just being married does not mean you or your spouse couldn't be subject to probate when the other dies. It all depends on how you've held your assets during your lifetime. If both of you pass away and you have minor children, 100% of your money and assets will be subject to probate.

In the next chapter, I'm going to walk you through what probate looks like so you know exactly what your loved ones would be dealing with.

CHAPTER EIGHT
Avoid Probate at All Costs!

This is probably not the most professional way to put this, but *probate sucks*.

Here are some key characteristics of probate, at least in states such as California:

- Probate is a very long process—it often lasts two years or more.

- Your money is frozen and is not immediately accessible for your children.

- Probate court is open and public, meaning anyone can go down to the court and see exactly what and how much you owned at the time of your death.

- Someone has to open up probate for your estate. They are stuck cleaning up your mess. Imagine that—you die unexpectedly and your family has to not only deal with your loss, but also get thrown into the court system for several years.

- Probate court is depressing, as are most court rooms in general. There is usually a "dog pound" of sad, depressed people in the halls who look like they are waiting to go into a torture chamber.

- Probate court is a platform for your family members to publicly air their grievances and argue over your children.

- And finally, probate court is very, very, and I mean VERY expensive.

What Probate Costs

The cost of probate varies depending on the state you live in and oftentimes the size of your estate.

In California, the probate code sets the cost for probate as a percentage of the total value of your estate. This percentage of your estate pays the attorney and the person administering your estate. On top of that there are court fees, costs, and potentially additional attorney's fees. We estimate for our clients that probate will cost them on average approximately 5% of their total estate worth (it could be less or more depending on the size and complexity of your estate).

This is usually when people will say: I don't own much. The bank basically owns my home and I've barely paid down the mortgage. I have a lot of student loans still and my retirement account doesn't have a lot in it. I have a life insurance policy, but that just goes to my spouse, and then to my kids, right?

Wrong. Wrong. Wrong.

Let me give you a simple scenario to help explain what probate could cost your family. Suppose you and your spouse passed away while your kids are still younger than eighteen. At the time of your death, your financial situation looks like this:

- Your Home: Your home has a market value of $750,000. You owe $640,000.

- Your Bank and Savings Accounts: You have about $15,000 in checking and $30,000 in savings.

- Your Stock: You have $15,000 worth of stock.

- Your Retirement Accounts: Your 401(k) has about $120,000. Your spouse does not have a 401(k).

- Your Life Insurance: You have a $1 million policy, and your spouse has a $250,000 policy.

- Your Debt: You still have about $60,000 in student loans and $15,000 on your Visa that you incurred when your spouse quit work after having a baby and before you got your promotion.

Probate court will base your total estate worth on the market value of your assets, not on your equity and not on your debt. This means for the couple I described above, their total estate worth would be as follows:

ASSET	FAIR MARKET VALUE
HOME	$750,000
CHECKING & SAVINGS	$45,000
STOCK	$15,000
RETIREMENT ACCOUNTS	$120,000
COMBINED LIFE INSURANCE	$1,250,000
TOTAL ESTATE WORTH	$2,180,000
YOUR PROBABTE COST (AT 5%)	**$109,000**

That's crazy, right? The probate cost for this couple who passed away is $109,000.

How Life Insurance and Retirement Accounts Are Brought into Probate Court

We talked earlier about what happens when someone is named as the beneficiary on a life insurance policy or retirement account—the money goes to them outright without any restrictions or protections. While many people do name their minor children as beneficiaries, children cannot receive any money outright until they are age eighteen. If they are not yet eighteen, the probate court has to step in and set up safeguards and custodians/guardians for their money since you did not.

Probate Lasts Even Longer If You Have Minor Children

If you have minor children, the nightmare of probate continues until your youngest child is eighteen. This is because the court usually will place whatever money is left (after the lawyers, courts, and fees are all paid) into blocked accounts for each minor child. Every year the appointed custodians/guardians of the account have to go back to court to show how the money is being used for the benefit of the children. Once a child turns eighteen, they get whatever is left in their blocked account, outright, without any restrictions. We'll talk later on about why this is detrimental to your kids and what you can do about it.

What Happens after Probate Is Completed

If probate sounds like a nightmare, well it really is. Even when it comes to an end, it can leave an emotional scar on your family for a lifetime.

I knew a very tight-knit family that had seven adult children. They came together when their mom died, but fell apart when the dad passed two years later. The father had left a will, but it was old, outdated, and boilerplate. In the will he split everything equally among his seven children. It seemed like it would be an easy process, just opening up probate and then splitting everything equally, but that was unfortunately not the case.

One of the adult children and her son had for years lived with the parents. Half of the siblings strongly believed that the father would have wanted that adult daughter and her son to continue to live in the family home, at least until the son was raised. The other half of the siblings felt that it was time for the adult daughter to start paying her own way and be on her own, and that the share of money the father left behind for her could help her get her own start. This family battled with each other in court, and when all was said and done, hardly anyone in the family was talking.

What was most devastating is that the situation could have been avoided had the father set up a proper estate plan, kept it up-to-date, and explained to the children why he was doing what he was. Maybe the adult children would not have agreed, but it would have avoided a battle over the question of what the dad really wanted. I think one thing they all agreed on in the end is that the parents never would have wanted the family to have been torn apart like it was. Even to this day, that family has never fully reconciled.

Are you leaving your family in a situation like this? By not planning, or by having poor planning, are you subjecting your family to the expense and hassle and heartache of probate?

I get so frustrated when I hear people say they just don't have time to do their estate planning. I know you truly love your family, so isn't setting up an estate plan worth your time when it means you can spare them from the grueling process of probate?

Arranging playdates, working out, doing homework, going to work, visiting a friend, cleaning your house, going on a date, looking at Facebook, and all of the other day-to-day things you get bogged down with are important, but not as important as taking the time to plan for the people you love.

CHAPTER NINE

The Best Way to Pass Your Money to Those You Love

Right now, without having created your own estate plan, your family would be locked into a probate nightmare that I know you don't want. You are probably wondering where the exit door is so you can make sure you don't end up there.

There is an escape from this! In fact, probate is completely voluntary—you only end up there if you choose to be there by your failure to act now.

The way you avoid the grueling process of probate is by setting up a revocable living trust. In the legal world, we describe a revocable living trust as a legal agreement that governs how, upon your death, your assets will pass to the people you've chosen to receive them. The street definition of a trust is that thing your lawyer sets up so your money doesn't end up going to the government to sort out.

When I explain what a trust is to clients, I tell them to think of an empty box. We call that empty box your trust. Now think of everything you own—your home, your bank accounts, your investment accounts, your personal belongings, anything that is yours. Visualize yourself placing all of these things inside that empty box. I explain that if you get a new couch or if you buy a new home, you can put it inside that box. And if you sell a couch or sell your home, it automatically goes outside of the box.

Now, let's say you suddenly die. That is when a lid is placed on top of the box, and anything inside of the box will privately and automatically pass according to your wishes. However, anything left outside of the box ends up in probate (we'll soon discuss how to make sure this does not happen to you).

A trust is actually a very easy way to make sure that your money automatically goes to your spouse or children instead of probate when you die. I know—it seems like magic, and it can be!

Here's the best part. Remember the enormous cost of probate, as we discussed earlier? The probate fee is completely eliminated when you set up your own estate planning that includes a revocable living trust.

You are probably wondering, why doesn't everyone just go and set up a trust-based estate plan? **The number one reason most people do not set up an estate plan is because they procrastinate.** So many people convince themselves they'll get around to setting up an estate plan next week, or next month, or before their next vacation, or when they get their next tax return refund, or when school is back in session . . . you may even have your own reason for not having done it.

Here is the hard truth, though: life does happen, people do die, and I bet the majority of people who die without having done their planning thought they would take care of it before it was too late.

If you want to make sure that your family can avoid probate and that the transfer of your money to those you love is done painlessly and privately, you need to set up a revocable living trust.

> A trust is actually a very easy way to make sure that your money goes to your spouse or children instead of probate when you die.

CHAPTER TEN

The #1 Reason Trusts Fail

I have educated you on why your family must have a re-vocable living trust and just how great it is when you have one. You are probably getting excited about the idea of having one set up for your family! I am going to have to take a little wind out of your sails though, because not all revocable living trusts will work the way you need them to. In fact, many trusts fail.

The number one reason that trusts fail is that people do not move their assets into their trust. Your assets will not automatically go into your trust just because you signed a legal document that said "trust" on it! Once your trust is created, you have to start moving your assets into that trust, and continue to do so every time you acquire a new asset (also known as "funding your trust"). Do not assume your attorney did or will do this for you.

Most attorneys tell their clients that they need to do this, but few people and their attorneys actually see this through. They fail to:

Change title on the deed for their home from their own name to the name of the trust.

Change the account holder name on their bank account to the name of the trust.

Change the backup beneficiary on their life insurance policy from their minor children's names to their trust.

Change the backup beneficiary on their retirement accounts from their minor children's names to the trusts created for their children.

In other words, they don't take the proper steps to put their stuff into the box! Thus, all the stuff left outside of the box ends up in probate.

Buyer beware! Never hire a law firm or anybody else to help you set up a trust if they are simply leaving it to you to put your assets into it yourself. You won't! Half of my clients who come to me with a trust already set up discover that their attorney only *mentioned* to them they needed to do this, rather than doing it for them or holding their hand and guiding them as they do it themselves.

The **worst** calls I get are from people who just lost a loved one and thought that they had their estate planning all set up, only to discover that none of the assets were moved into the trust. They are crushed! They thought all along this had been taken care of, only to discover it wasn't and there is now nothing they can do about it.

Make sure you work with a firm that has a process that will not let this happen to your family. They must have a tight process in place for helping you connect your assets to your trust, and continue to guide you throughout your lifetime as you acquire new accounts and property. This is where the true value of having a real relationship with your attorney comes in.

CHAPTER ELEVEN

Passing Money to Your Spouse

When I talk with clients about how they want their money to go to the surviving spouse, oftentimes one of them will glare at the other spouse like they're saying *don't you even think about giving my money away to some lover*! We call it the "pool boy" scenario, where the rich wife runs off with a poor, handsome, younger lover who is really just after the late husband's wealth.

When you set up a trust, you can decide how you want your money to go to your spouse when you die. That is the beauty of having a trust—it avoids probate and allows you to determine how your surviving spouse can use your money.

There are two popular options for passing money through your trust to your spouse. One way is to just give it to your spouse outright, which is similar to what happens when you own an asset jointly or name your spouse as a beneficiary on a policy. The second option is to pass the money to your spouse so he or she can always benefit from it, and maybe even manage it if you want, but the money stays protected from third parties.

Option One: Giving Your Spouse the

Money Free and Clear

Many people like the concept of just giving everything to their surviving spouse when the first of them dies, allowing the surviving spouse to do whatever they want with it. It works very similarly to when you pass money through joint ownership or by naming your spouse as beneficiary on a policy.

The benefit of passing money this way is that it allows extreme flexibility since your spouse receives the money free and clear.

The downside is because they can do what they want with it and have the final say over how it is spent, they can give it away to a new spouse or someone other than your children. They could also risk losing it if they were sued, divorced, or preyed upon.

Option Two: Giving Your Spouse Money with Restrictions and Protections

You may really like the idea of giving your spouse your share of the money, but may not necessarily want your spouse to have the power to spend it however he or she wants or give it away to someone other than your children.

You also may want to protect your spouse from the risk of losing the money to ill-intentioned people.

There are several techniques that attorneys can use to provide for this type of protection, but the technique our office generally prefers is called the **Clayton Election**. The Clayton Election allows a spouse to leave money behind for the continued support of the surviving spouse (including health, education, maintenance, and support), but prevents them from using the money for other purposes, like paying off creditors or judgments, or giving it away to people other than the beneficiaries you both agreed upon.

Many couples are less concerned about their spouse doing something bad with the money and more concerned it could be lost to ill-intentioned third parties. They want their spouse to have lots of flexibility in how the money is used, but don't want them to give it away or have it taken from them.

This type of arrangement is called a **beneficiary controlled asset protection trust**. I really like this setup because you are essentially giving your surviving spouse complete control, yet protecting that money from other people. They will have many options for protecting that money if they are ever facing a divorce, lawsuit, bankruptcy, creditor, or any other outside threat.

What's best for you and your spouse largely depends on your goals and situation. Working with a well-respected attorney who is familiar with asset protection trusts and marital relationships can help you make the best decision for your family.

CHAPTER TWELVE

Passing Money to Your Children

A few years ago I met with a young woman who had just had her first son. I asked what brought her in to get her estate planning in place, assuming she'd say guardianship, but for her, that wasn't it. She said, "I'm here because I never want to burden my son with money."

I was thinking, *That sounds like a great problem to have!*

But in reality it wasn't. She told me that when she was eighteen years old, she received a very large inheritance, outright and without any restrictions. She was extremely bright, but instead of going to college as she had planned and doing all of the things most of us do in our twenties to build our futures, she ended up traveling and attracting the wrong people. It all came to halt when she found out she was expecting a child. By the time she came in to see me, all of the money was gone. She was starting over from scratch. She taught me an important lesson:

Passing money to your children at the wrong time (too young), and in the wrong way (without restrictions) creates a burden rather than a blessing.

I know you would never want your children to experience the pain and heartache our client did because of sudden wealth. The good news is that you can keep this from happening by passing money through a trust that is properly structured and managed. A trust allows you to create the terms for how you want to provide for your children and who you want to manage the money on their behalf.

There are three popular types of beneficiary trusts that you will likely want to use: common trusts, stated age trusts, and lifetime asset protection trusts.

Common Trusts

If you have more than one child and they are all under eighteen, it makes a lot of sense to keep your money for them all together to be used for their health, education, maintenance, and support. This type of structure, which the legal world calls a **common trust**, allows the adult in charge of the money to draw from one shared pot of money. It mirrors what we are doing now for our children while we are alive.

For example, my daughter was recently injured and needed a few stitches in her head (we never did get a straight story from her brothers on how this happened). The hospital bill was very expensive. Her needs that month cost us much more than our other children's needs because of her injury. Thus, we financially benefited our daughter more than our sons that month. This is what happens when you have a common trust. While all the children's needs are met, the amount of money used on each child may be unequal.

At some point, after the kids are raised and become more independent, the common trust should end. You can decide the appropriate age for that to happen, at which point the remaining money will be divided up and transferred into separate trusts for each child, which we'll look at below. We usually recommend the common trust terminate when the youngest turns eighteen, or, if the family is college-minded, then when the youngest turns twenty-three or graduates from college, whichever occurs first.

Stated Age Trusts

After the common trust terminates, the remaining assets can be divided into separate **stated age trusts** for each of your children. While the assets are in the separate trusts, your trustee will use the assets for your children's benefit. But when each child reaches certain ages or milestones, you can instruct the trustee to distribute all or a portion of the trust assets to your child outright without restrictions. You can do this all in one lump sum or you can distribute a percentage of the trust assets at stated ages (e.g., at age twenty-five the child gets 25% of the trust assets, at age thirty the child gets 50% of the trust assets, and at age thirty-five the child gets the remaining trust assets).

My clients often ask, what is a good age for my children to get full access to their money? Because many of their children are so young, it is difficult for them to know how their child will be as an adult. Some things to consider are:

- The trust always pays for your child's health, education, maintenance, and support, so really what you're determining is at what age you want your child—rather than the adult who was put in charge of the money—to control the money and spend it.

- Brain development does not end until age twenty-five. Any age younger than that is a bad idea.

- People experience many platonic and romantic relationships in their twenties, and many of your child's peers will not yet have their own money and success in their twenties. You don't want your child to stand out as the rich kid and thus attract people to them for the wrong reasons. Hopefully, once your child and their peers hit their thirties, they will all be on more equal footing since their peers will have become more self-sufficient and settled down.

- The twenties is a time when people develop tremendously (at lease it should be!). You don't want money waiting in the wings to deter your children from graduating from college and establishing their own career and independence.

As you can see, I am not a big fan of people getting money in their twenties. Clients usually ask, what about a wedding, or starting a business, or a home? You can structure your trust to allow the adult in charge of your child's money to use trust money to pay for these important things and anything else you want; it just means that the adult gets to use discretion on what amount is appropriate for these purposes, rather than giving your child free reign.

Once your child hits the age you've chosen for them to receive their money, the money is fully theirs, outright and clear. This means they can spend it, lose it, invest it, use it on other people, or give it away however they want. The assets are also subject to creditors, predators, and divorce.

Lifetime Asset Protection Trusts

The **lifetime asset protection trust** allows you to provide for your child's health, education, maintenance, support, and anything else you allow, but, unlike the stated age trust, the money stays protected in the trust for your child's lifetime. The power of the lifetime asset protection trust is that the money is always available for your child's benefit, but it is protected from improper or wasteful spending and from the outside world (e.g., creditors, predators, and divorce). Given how prevalent divorce and lawsuits are in society today, there is a good chance that at least one of your children and their assets will be subject to third-party threats. A lifetime asset protection trust is one of the few options available to protect their inheritance against the outside world. This is the type of trust I have chosen for my own children.

There are two ways to set up a lifetime asset protection trust for your child.

One option is to make another adult in charge of the money for your child's entire lifetime, so while the child benefits from the money, they never actually control it. Some clients don't like the idea because they feel it is too controlling. Other clients, who already know that their child will never become responsible enough to manage their own money, like this arrangement.

The other option is to set the trust up so your child will always benefit from the trust, but at some point will actually get to control it as well. Many people find this arrangement ideal because it provides their child both freedom and protections.

I also encourage my clients to create **lifetime trust distribution guidelines**, which provide further guidance and instruction to your trustee on how you would like your assets to be used for your child. You can also create incentives for pursuing certain business, career, educational, family, or philanthropic endeavors, or anything else you would like to encourage your child to pursue or explore. The idea is to provide the same guidance, support, and encouragement to your child that you would if you were still alive.

The best trust for your child is the one that sets your child up for success. I encourage you to talk with an attorney who has a lot of experience in this area who can guide you into making the best decision for your particular child.

CHAPTER THIRTEEN

Providing for Children with Disabilities

If you have a child with a disability, I want to help give you some guidance and comfort because I know you really worry about who is going to care for and love your child the special way you do now. Even if you don't have a child with a disability, I hope you read this chapter. I'm sure you have a friend whose child has autism, Down syndrome, cerebral palsy, or another disability, and I want to pass on some insights into their lives so you can be an even better friend and support to them.

I have helped many families set up comprehensive estate plans that protect their child with a disability. I also have met many families that have a child with a disability through our local United Cerebral Palsy Center, which my family is involved with both professionally and personally. Here's what I've learned about parents who have a child with a disability:

You have a deep, sacrificial love for your child. You (or your spouse) gave up a career to become a full-time caretaker. You go back and forth between endless appointments, evaluations, and therapy, and on top of that you have to battle insurance companies, the school system, and other obstacles just to get your child support.

I know it's been tough for you emotionally. You've probably felt misunderstood, rejected, or isolated by your family members and friends at times.

And I know you really, really love your child. You worry about who will be there for your child the way you are now.

Planning is one of the best ways to ensure that your child with a disability will always be cared for and provided for in the best possible way. Most of the concepts in this book will help you do that, but there are some additional things you'll need to consider when you set up an estate plan.

1. Your Child's Physical Care

Make sure that, in addition to naming temporary and permanent guardians, you include guidance on how to physically care for your child so their services and care are not disrupted or neglected should something happen to you.

At our firm, we actually send these instructions out in advance to temporary or permanent guardians so they would know what to do if your child were suddenly placed in their care.

2. Your Child's Financial Care

Your child may be entitled to valuable government benefits now or in the future because of his or her disability. Unfortunately, most of these benefits are available only to those with very limited means. This leaves you in a difficult position: leaving your child an inheritance could actually disqualify him or her from receiving important government benefits they would have otherwise been entitled to.

Fortunately, you can establish a special needs trust that allows you to leave your child an inheritance in a way that does not disqualify him or her from receiving government benefits. Because special needs trusts are established for the purpose of supplementing government benefits, government benefits can cover your child's basic needs while the special needs trust pays for additional needs.

It can also be set up so that, should your child no longer need a special need trust, they can receive their money either through a stated age trust or lifetime asset protection trust.

3. Your Child's Emotional Care

You are an integral part of your child's life; you provide physical, emotional, and financial care. It's natural to worry about your child's emotional needs and care, especially if something should happen to you and you could no longer care for them.

One great way to express your love for your child and help ensure that their emotional needs will continue to be met is to create a **Memorandum of Intent**. This legal document allows you to outline your child's emotional needs and provide your insight to guide future caretakers in how to meet these needs.

Lastly, I want you to make sure you work with an attorney who is highly skilled at developing plans that meet the needs of your child with a disability, but also equally able to meet the needs of all of the other family members. You never want to work with a lawyer who places a disproportionate emphasis on one family member, or who does not have the legal skill set required to properly set up a special needs trust.

How would you like to learn how to fully protect your child with a disability?

Visit meierevents.com to register for our 10 Legal Protections For Children With Disabilities Workshop, or call Meier Law Firm at 949.718.0420 for details.

CHAPTER FOURTEEN

Dealing with Your Ex

I hope you can skip over this chapter, but if not, you are part of a large group of parents who have to deal with an ex-spouse or ex-partner who is the other legal parent of your child.

Setting up an estate plan is even more necessary for you because, if you leave it to the default laws, your money will not pass the way you want to your current spouse and children, and your ex could potentially end up controlling—and even one day inheriting—the money you left behind for the child you share. You also risk your extended family being cut out of your child's life if your ex becomes the sole guardian and refuses to facilitate visits.

I know I just listed a lot of fears you probably have, but I am going to help you mitigate them.

Guardianship and Visitation

This is probably not what you want to hear, but your ex-spouse or ex-partner who is the legal parent of your child will automatically have sole guardianship of your child when you pass away, unless guardianship is contested and a court deems your ex to be unfit. A court's standard of "unfit" is as low as it goes, so unless your ex is legally forbidden from seeing them now, or subsequent events warrant this, it is unlikely anyone in your family could successfully contest them being sole guardian.

This happened recently in the Paul Walker case. You'll recall Paul Walker was a famous actor who was killed in an accident in 2013 and left behind a teenage daughter, Meadow. Meadow had lived with Paul Walker's mother before the actor's death. When Paul died, Meadow's grandmother filed a petition for guardianship of Meadow, which was contested by Meadow's mother (who was not married to Paul Walker). Meadow's mother claimed she had the legal right to be sole guardian, while Meadow's grandmother claimed she was unfit due to issues with alcohol. The case eventually settled and Meadow's mother was granted custody.

I know that the thought of your children having to go with your ex, especially if you have been the one primarily raising them, is terrifying. While that is probably out of your control, **it's important that your estate plan include your wishes for liberal visitation so your family can see your child if you pass away.** Many states allow grandparent, stepparent, and sibling visitation, so make sure you express your strong desire for a court to allow visitation if your ex will not.

Money

You can make sure your ex never financially benefits from the money you leave behind by passing your money to your shared child in the right way. We've talked in earlier chapters about the danger of passing money through probate, because then a judge will place the money in a blocked account. Guess who they could appoint to be in charge of that money? Your child's guardian . . . your ex!

The best practice is to pass the money through a trust and appoint another adult to manage the money so there is plenty of oversight on how the money is being used for your child.

There's also the concern that, if you pass money to your child through probate or through a stated age trust and then your child predeceases your ex, your ex could inherit their money as your child's heir at law.

You can prevent this from happening if you pass your money to your child through a lifetime asset protection trust, and authorize the money be left only to your grandchildren, or to someone else you have chosen, when your child passes away.

Legacy Preservation

I hope that if something happened to you that your ex would help keep your memory alive, but you really should not trust anyone to do this. Read about the Legacy Interview because it is even more important for you to make sure you have preserved who you are so you can always be a presence in your child's life.

Goodwill

I believe your best chance for ensuring that your child would continue a great relationship with everyone in their life if you passed away, is to start doing today whatever you can to create a more amicable and supportive relationship with your ex.

In many cases building goodwill with an ex feels undeserved and impossible. I know there is a lot of ongoing pain caused by your ex or by the experience of having to start over. My heart sincerely goes out to you and all parents stuck in this tough situation. It is not easy.

Let me encourage you to keep being the best you, even if the situation is unfair. Trust and believe that the goodwill you build today will somehow find its way into your child's tomorrow. I have seen this happen for other families and believe it can happen for yours.

Stop Worrying

I am going to include this point because I know you worry a lot about the concerns addressed in this chapter. Unless you are knowingly facing the prospect of death right now, stop worrying about this scenario because it is very unlikely that you will die while your child is young.

Trust and believe that the goodwill you build today will somehow find its way into your child's tomorrow.

CHAPTER FIFTEEN

How to Avoid Estate Taxes

No one likes taxes. They seem to be a problem for everyone. My husband had an IRS agent tell him that taxes were even a problem for her. She told him that no one wants to date her because of who she works for!

Most people don't like the idea of loved ones having to pay estate taxes on the money they leave behind, especially since they already paid taxes on that money while they were alive. Some believe that the government is double dipping.

Fortunately, right now the federal government will allow you to pass a little over five million dollars tax-free to someone else when you die.[1] Married couples can pass an unlimited amount to the spouse upon death, which is even better.

If your assets add up to more than five million dollars, there are over 200 tools to help you reduce or eliminate estate taxes, but you have to take advantage of them.

Remember Phillip Seymour Hoffman? He passed away unexpectedly and had not updated his will in over ten years.

---

[1] It's important to find out what your state law says about estate taxes, since those taxes could apply to you.

Because he did not take advantage of strategies to reduce his taxes, his family is facing a $15 million estate tax bill that he could have significantly reduced through proper planning.

I have personally had new clients who have come to me after losing someone they love, only to realize that I cannot help them after the fact avoid paying taxes on the money that was left for them. I can only help them going forward.

If your family will face an estate tax problem when you die, you need to talk with a highly skilled attorney who can help you reduce taxes. **However,** you have to make sure that whoever is helping you does not place a dispro-portionate emphasis on tax avoidance, neglecting other important considerations we've discussed, like creating an emergency plan and asset protection for your children.

Also, the government changes its rules on how much estate money you can pass tax-free, which is all the more reason to make sure you are working with a trusted advisor who is helping you monitor these laws and keep your plan up-to-date. Our firm has been fortunate to work with some of the best tax attorneys in the country who have co-counseled with us when creating plans for extremely wealthy families with young children. You can have a child-centered estate plan and avoid taxes too!

CHAPTER SIXTEEN

What about Your Digital Assets?

It used to be that all of our photos and memoirs were inside a treasure chest for only us and our close friends to see. Nowadays, we have ourselves and our kids plastered all over the Internet and use that as the baby book we never quite got around to finishing (at least for the second child).

We also used to have to use paper money or checks to pay bills, go inside a bank or company to make transactions, and call or send letters to update or change account information. Now, there is an online account for almost everything (banking, utilities, life insurance, retirement accounts, etc.), and most payments are made online. In fact, many institutions don't even have a brick and mortar location—they can be accessed only online. Often one spouse takes the lead on paying bills and handling online accounts. Would your spouse even know what accounts you have, let alone know your login information to access them?

So what happens to your social media (Facebook, Instagram, LinkedIn, Google+, and every other social media platform you post on) and your online banking and transactional accounts if something happens to you? That largely depends on what you've done beforehand to spell out your wishes.

In estate plans you designate a person to be in charge of handling your assets when you die so that bills get paid and money is transferred to the people you gave it to. But many estate plans fail to address what should happen to your *digital* assets or how to access those assets if they are in online accounts. An estate plan that doesn't address this modern norm is, well, quite archaic!

When you address your digital assets, be sure to consider:

- Who you want to be in charge of your social media accounts

- What you want to happen to your social media accounts

- How the appropriate people can access your social media accounts

- Who you want to inherit your digital assets

- What banking and institutional accounts are online and how can they be accessed

You may remember Stieg Larsson, the late author of the best-selling "Millennium" crime series that began with *The Girl with the Dragon Tattoo*. His fourth book was left unfinished on his laptop when he died suddenly in 2004 at age fifty. He was not married to his partner, and under the default laws all of his assets went to his family. His partner and his family became involved in a major legal dispute over who should own the rights to the unfinished book.

Make sure your estate plan addresses what happens to your digital assets. We use a **Virtual Asset Instructions Letter** that helps clients direct how their virtual assets are handled.

CHAPTER SEVENTEEN
Why Medical Directives Really Matter

When you had your first child and were at the hospital doing the pre-op work, you may recall the hospital asking if you had any medical directives. Without having your own medical directives, there are many questions left unanswered about your physical care and support. By not having legally declared your wishes, should something happen to you, your loved ones would be in the ultimate nightmare situation.

I was out walking a few years ago with one of my sons when my cell phone rang. It was a longtime friend whom I had not heard from in some time, so I took the call. I can still clearly remember standing on the side of the main road in my neighborhood with my son in his stroller. It seemed like I was standing there for an eternity as I processed what she was saying to me.

She skipped the "hi, how are you" part and immediately began with, "I don't know if you heard, but Joe [name changed] was in a very bad accident."

My heart sunk. I could not believe what I was hearing.

"It's very serious," she continued. "The doctors are talking to me about removing him from life support. I don't know what to do."

Her husband was in his late thirties. Their son was just a little boy. They were normal people just like you and me. And, in a flash, due to a serious accident, their lives were forever changed. The fact that Joe's wishes were not legally known added to the great stress already placed on his young family.

You may remember the Terri Schiavo case in the 1990s to 2005. Terri Schiavo was a beautiful young woman who had a heart attack that caused major damage to her brain due to a lack of oxygen. After two and a half months in a coma, her doctors labeled her condition a "persistent vegetative state."

Terri Schiavo did not have a living will. Sadly, her husband and her parents did not agree on whether she should be artificially kept alive in the state she was in, and for fifteen years they battled in court on whether she should be removed from life support. Ultimately, Terri Schiavo's life support was terminated and she passed away. This was the ultimate nightmare situation that could have been avoided had Terri Schiavo made her wishes legally known.

Have you left your spouse in a situation where he or she won't know exactly what you want? I hope not. I don't ever want a situation like Terri Shiavo's to happen to you or your spouse. Keep this from happening to you by making your wishes legally known.

CHAPTER EIGHTEEN
How to Make Your Medical Wishes Known

My friend's situation shows just how important it is to make our medical wishes known. There are three main documents you will need to do this: a living will, an advanced health care directive, and a HIPAA authorization. I'll discuss all three of them.

Living Will

A living will is a legal declaration that states your end of life wishes.

Most living wills state that, should you fall into a permanent vegetative state or have a terminal illness or incurable condition, your life shall not be artificially prolonged. This statement is subject to certain guidelines you dictate. In other words, a living will declares that if there's really no chance you can ever recover, then you want your family to let you go. It's your wishes for your end of life care.

Some people actually want to declare the opposite. They want to be artificially kept alive, even if there is no chance of recovery.

It's important for you to make your wishes clear. Talk with your doctor and attorney about what makes the most sense for you.

Advanced Health Care Directive

An **Advanced Health Care Directive** (also known as a Health Care Power of Attorney) works in conjunction with your living will and allows you to designate someone to make and carry out your medical decisions for you if you are incapacitated. It provides instructions on your medical evaluation and treatment, long-term care and hospice, your wishes on staying in your residence versus a facility, who can hire and fire your doctors, and your wishes when it comes to pain relief, psychiatric treatment, organ donation, and other important decisions that must be made should you become incapacitated.

Don't leave your family in a position where it's unclear who you want to make medical decisions for you. Maybe you think it would be clear you want your spouse, but what if your spouse couldn't do it? What if your spouse was also injured or was simply not in a mental state to make decisions for you when needed? An Advanced Health Care Directive addresses all of these scenarios, and every person needs one.

HIPAA Authorization

You probably already know that your medical information is private. If I called your doctor and asked for a copy of your latest medical exam, they'd tell me I can't have it. This is because Congress passed a law known as the Health Insurance Portability and Accountability Act (HIPAA). It limits use, disclosure, or release of your health information.

It makes sense that a stranger should not be able to call your doctor and get sensitive medical information about you, but what if I was your best friend and had just rushed down to the hospital because I heard you had been in an accident. Shouldn't I be able to at least find out what happened to you?

The answer is no, unless you have authorized me to receive that type of information in an emergency situation.

So, in light of HIPAA, what can you do if there are actually people that you love and trust who you would want doctors to be able to talk to if you were in a serious medical condition and could not communicate? You can execute a HIPAA authorization form, where you list the names of individuals you are authorizing your doctor to talk to.

If you have not yet completed a HIPAA authorization form, you should. We recommend that, in addition to your spouse and backup decision makers, you should authorize key friends or family members who could help relay word of your condition to the people who love and care about you. You will also want to make sure that any of your financial decision makers are listed so if you are incapacitated they use your assets for your benefit.

I had a client once who, when asked who she wanted on her HIPAA list, requested that I list every woman in her book group. I said, "Don't you think if we listed one of them that she could get the word out to the others?" My client said, "Yeah, but I don't want anyone to feel left out."

I had a good laugh over that request. While you may not need your whole book group on your HIPAA list, you definitely need to make sure your key contacts and loved ones are.

CHAPTER NINETEEN

Special Considerations for Mothers

There has been a lot of attention in the media lately over women who have fallen into a vegetative state while pregnant. Through modern medicine and technology, doctors may be able to save an unborn child even when the mother becomes incapacitated. It may be a situation you or your spouse has never contemplated, but it's one that women in their childbearing years should definitely address.

Would you want to be artificially kept alive in a permanent vegetative state if you were pregnant? I ask my female clients this question. If they answer yes, we include a "pregnancy override clause" in their living will that states they would not want to be removed from life support if they were pregnant and the doctors determined the baby could develop properly and be safely delivered.

Recently, there was a family in Texas who had to face this awful situation. The wife, who was expecting the couple's second child, became brain-dead while fourteen weeks pregnant. The woman had not legally made her medical wishes known.

The woman's husband wanted his wife to be removed from life support. He stated that his wife would not have wanted to be kept alive in that state. Medical reports indicated his unborn child was not developing properly, likely because the mother had been deprived of oxygen before she became brain-dead.

However, Texas had a controversial law that forbade the hospital from removing the woman from life support because she was pregnant. Thus, even if the woman had a medical directive that stated she would not want to be artificially kept alive in that condition, it would not have overrode state law.

Most states allow women to decide whether they would want to be artificially kept alive if they fell into an irreversible vegetative condition while pregnant. Even if your state does not give you the ultimate discretion, you should still make your wishes known and clear.

When you consider this difficult issue, you need to work with an attorney who understands all of the possible ramifications of your decision, such as:

- What laws, if any, does your state have regarding pregnancy and incapacity?

- What if you were early in your pregnancy?

- What if the doctors determined your unborn child was not developing properly because of the event that caused your irreversible vegetative condition?

- Would you want your spouse to ultimately make the call, or would you want your family to have to abide by your preset wishes?

- What do your moral beliefs and conscience dictate when pregnancy and incapacity collide?

I have found that a woman's position on elective abortion has no bearing on whether she feels compelled to be kept on artificial life support while pregnant.

Women should discuss the pregnancy override clause with their spouse, attorney, spiritual leader, or other trusted advisors before making their wishes legally known.

CHAPTER TWENTY

Why Most Medical Directives Don't Work

I usually ask the crowd at my speaking engagements how many of them have medical directives. I estimate that 15% of the crowd usually raises a hand.

Then I say, "Of those of you who raised your hand, how many of you can access your medical directives right now from where you are sitting?" That's when all of the hands go down. This is huge problem.

Having medical directives is not good enough. You have to make sure they are always accessible.

I once got a call from a client. She said her husband was searching his father's office trying to hunt down his medical directives. Meanwhile, the father was at the local hospital having emergency triple bypass heart surgery. She said to me, "I know how to access our directives, but do you have any idea where other people might store theirs?"

Too many times, people have medical directives that become completely useless because their family cannot access them during their time of crises. This puts the family back at square one where no one has any idea who should be the decision maker, whether they had a living will, or who the hospital can talk to.

In modern times, there is no reason that clients should not have their medical directives accessible. For our clients, we store medical directives on a secure online database, and they carry cards in their wallets and provide copy cards to their designated decision makers, so that at any time, no matter where they are in the world, their decision makers can access their medical directives.

If you have medical directives already or plan to get them, make sure they are accessible, anytime, anywhere—no exception. Remember, 100% of emergencies are not planned, but they can be planned for!

Too many times, people have medical directives that become completely useless because their family cannot access them during this time of crisis.

CHAPTER TWENTY ONE

How to Never Say Goodbye

This is by far the hardest chapter to write. I hope you stick with me through this.

I am a mother of young children like you, and I know that if something happened to me right now, my children would not really remember me.

They would not remember the stories I've told them about the day I met their dad and the line of the century he told me when we sat down for dinner.

They would not remember the stories I've told them about what I felt the first time I saw them on the ultrasound and then on the day they were born.

They would not remember the thousands of hugs and kisses I've given them (and hopefully not the many times I've yelled at them!).

They would not remember the times I've comforted them or encouraged them or told them they are amazing and special.

They would not remember all of the times I've sat in the crowd waving at them while they sang their hearts out at their school performance, or what it took for me to get there.

They would not remember all of the things I have told them about being a good person and following their heart—that no matter what they do right or wrong, God loves them unconditionally, and they are His beautiful child.

And there are so many conversations we've yet to have about life, relationships, decisions, and roads to travel. There are many milestones they've yet to reach that I so much hope to be a part of.

If something did happen to me, I know that my little kids probably would not remember me. And that hurts. I would never want them to lose me, and I know they would never want to lose me either. But unfortunately, I can only control so much.

I know my husband would keep my memory alive, and my family would as well. Of course. Yes, I've posted hundreds of pictures of them on Facebook and shared inspirational quotes that reflect my beliefs and passions.

But deep within our hearts we all have so many special memories and dreams for our children that would be lost if something happened to us, simply because we have not yet shared them or because their little minds would forget.

I grew up with a girl who lost her mother to cancer when she was only eleven years old. Her father remarried shortly thereafter and life seemed to continue on, but as the girl continued to grow, there was always a piece of her missing—her mother.

Eventually the girl married a wonderful man. He wanted to give her a very special Christmas present shortly after they married. Without her knowing, he contacted several of her late mother's friends and asked them to write down a memory of his wife's late mother so he could compile them in a book for his wife. It was touching and beautiful that he took the time to give his wife something so special—something she had longed to have. It was also a painful reminder that after all those years, this girl still longed to know who her mother was.

What would you want your children to remember if your tomorrow never came? What do you think they would need to hear from you in the years to come?

One of the special things we do for the families we work with is a **Legacy Interview**. It's a one-hour audio-recorded interview in which parents answer questions they've preselected from a list we've given them. The Legacy Interview questions cover topics from important memories, instructions to your children's guardians, financial attitudes, religion, relationship advice, lessons learned, and many other important aspects of one's life and parenting.

Through the Legacy Interview, parents have the opportunity to preserve everything they hold dear in their hearts so their children can always remember them.

You can be part of your daughter's wedding day, even if you're gone.

You can speak words of encouragement to your child when they're struggling, even if you're gone.

You can laugh about the day you met your spouse, even if you're gone.

You can tell your spouse that you want them to be happy and find love again.

And you can say "I love you" one last time. Saying it today is important. Preserving it forever is a gift that can last their lifetime.

The truth is I didn't get into estate planning because I had a burning desire to save families from having to go through probate or pay extra fees. I got into estate planning because I wanted to help parents build a stronger, more intentional family and create a lasting love that can never be taken away by anyone or anything. I've done a Legacy Interview for my own kids and am so grateful they will have my love with them forever.

You don't even need to wait to do your estate planning to do a Legacy Interview. Do it now. For those of you who think this would be too painful or difficult to do, if nothing else, just record yourself saying "I love you." I promise you that your children will play it their entire lifetime.

CHAPTER TWENTY TWO

What Would You Change?

To recap, right now, without having created your own estate plan, you are subject to the plan created for you by your state.

This means that as of right now, if something happens to you, your plan is as follows:

- Your children will be placed in temporary foster care immediately following your death.

- Your children will have to go through a long and uncertain court process until a judge decides who should raise them.

- Your family will try and get some type of temporary legal custody so your children can get out of temporary foster care and stay with them until a judge makes a final decision.

- Someone in your family—not necessarily the person you would have chosen—will try and find an attorney to help open up a court case to access your money.

- Someone in your family will have to pay for your kids while all of your money is frozen during a long and expensive court process.

- Someone will need to hunt down all of your accounts so the court will know what you own (assuming they can even find all of your accounts).

- Roughly 5% of your total estate worth (including life insurance money, since your kids are too young to receive it) will be paid toward court costs alone.

- Everyone and their mother will have access to your private financial matters through open and public court records.

- Whatever money is left after a two-year court process will be placed into a blocked account that your children's guardians cannot freely access.

- Your children's guardians will have to hire an attorney and go back to court every year to show a judge how they are spending the money.

- A judge will pick a person to manage your kids' money, and this person may be someone you've never even met or even an ex-spouse.

- On their eighteenth birthdays your children will receive their inheritance outright, free and clear, without a single restriction.

- In their young adult life your child will be able to spend their inheritance on whatever they want, with no requirement whatsoever that they go to college or build their own financial security.

- Your child's boyfriend or girlfriend or whoever they want may benefit from your child's inheritance.

- Your surviving spouse will risk losing your share of the money to a future divorce or creditor instead of passing it on to the children.

- Your money may be lost to estate taxes instead of going to your spouse and kids.

- Your spouse and family members will not legally know what your wishes are if you've fallen into a permanent vegetative state.

- Your doctors will not know who they can legally talk to about your condition if you are seriously injured.

- You will not have a trusted person designated to make medical decisions regarding your treatment if you cannot make them for yourself.

- Your loved ones will not have any way to access your medical and financial wishes if you are incapacitated or have died.

- You cannot tell your children about the day they were born.

- You cannot tell your children on their wedding day that you wish them love and happiness.

- You cannot tell your spouse or children one last time that you love them.

- You cannot say goodbye until you meet again.

Let me ask you—out of that list, if you had to pick <u>one</u> thing to change, what would it be? Go back and read the list again. I know you probably would want to change most, if not all, of the consequences listed above, but you have to pick one.

If you are a mom, I am guessing that you don't like the idea of your children being placed in temporary foster care or having a judge determine who raises them.

If you are a dad, I am guessing you do not like the idea of your children getting their inheritance outright at age eighteen without any restrictions. Guardianship was probably a very close second for you.

This is your plan if you don't take the steps necessary to create your own plan. I know you don't want this, and I don't either.

It's time to change this for your family.

How would you like to get your estate plan set up for your family?

Visit meierfirm.com to schedule a planning session, or call Meier Law Firm at 949.718.0420 for more information. Sessions can be conducted at our offices in Newport Beach, CA or virtually.

CHAPTER TWENTY THREE
It's Time to Plan

Reading this book is a great first step for looking into your estate planning, and I hope you have found it educational and motivating. I want to help you build on that momentum by encouraging you to commit to getting a plan in place for your family.

When should you start to plan? Today.

Estate planning is the starting point for ensuring that the great life you've created for your family can never be taken away. If you don't take the time to do it now, everything you've built can be lost.

I know you have a lot going on this week, and next week, and this year, and next year, which is why it is imperative for you to take the time to get a plan now—so all of those great things can still happen, even if something happens to you. Today is the best day to plan for your great future and the futures of all of the people you love.

If you are ready to get your planning started and need to get connected with the right attorney, I invite you to connect with Meier Law Firm and see if we can assist you. Our greatest strength is the level of service and guidance we provide families like yours. If we are not the best fit, we can connect you with another reputable lawyer who can help.

I've also provided some bonus chapters to educate you on your options for having an estate plan put together and why it's imperative to work with a trusted attorney who regularly guides families with young children. I have included an Attorney Checklist so you can properly evaluate your prospective attorney before you hire them.

As this book comes to a close, let me leave you with this:

You're probably not going to die for a very long time.

I hope you plan for your kids because you love them, not out of fear of death.

Enjoy your life knowing that, no matter what, you've done everything you can to set your family up for the best.

Build the legacy you want to leave behind by living a better life today.

And finally, stop worrying and start your estate planning today!

About the Author

LAURA K MEIER, ESQ., is a top California business and estate planning attorney dedicated to guiding families with young children. She is the Founding Partner at Meier Law Firm, which she co-owns with her husband, Joshua D. Meier, Esq. The Meiers frequently speak, write, and counsel parents on how to meet their financial, legal, and moral obligations to their children through proper estate planning.

Laura is a graduate of J. Reuben Clark Law School at Brigham Young University. She worked for a national law firm before forming Meier Law Firm in 2010. Laura serves on the Board of Directors for the United Cerebral Palsy Orange County, and is a member of Wealth Counsel, LLC and Personal Family Lawyer®. Laura's work has been featured by NBC, ABC, CBS, FOX, and other national media outlets, and she has been honored twice by OC Metro Magazine as a top five attorney.

Most importantly, Laura and Joshua are the proud parents of four young children—Conrad, Jack, Kate, and Andrew. They live in Newport Beach, California, where Meier Law Firm is located.

For more information about Meier Law Firm and for free and important additional resources, please visit meierfirm. com or call 949.718.0420.

Who is the Right Lawyer to Help Your Family?

Hopefully after reading this book you feel much more educated on what type of estate plan your family needs. Now it's time to understand your options for putting a plan in place.

If you've already done some research, you've probably found that your options are to either hire a traditional attorney at a law firm, or do your own planning online. You probably felt that neither one seemed like a perfect option, right?

At my Kids Guardian Workshops I hear time and time again from parents with young children that they knew they needed to do their estate planning, but just couldn't find the right person or service to help them. **That's because 99% of the resources for estate planning were not designed for families with young children.**

Option One: The Traditional Attorney

I worked for a major law firm before I founded Meier Law Firm in 2010. Big law firms share common characteristics, which is why there are so many true lawyer jokes out there.

Most people try to avoid working with attorneys and for good reason. I don't want to give you the impression that big law firm attorneys are bad people or even bad attorneys. I was once practicing law just like them. And, like them, I just accepted that the practice of law was what it was, and there wasn't anything I could do about it.

If you have hired a big law firm to help you before, all of this is going to sound very familiar to you.

The typical client. For big estate planning law firms, the typical client is either elderly or wealthy. These are the people who have cash on hand to spend on an estate plan, and time to set one up. Families with young kids aren't the big law firms' focus because most families can't afford their fees, and they are harder to motivate because death seems far away. They're also too busy to come in.

All estate planning attorneys know that a young family should have estate planning; it's just that they don't see families come through their door every day. If the big firm does get a client with young children, they get a plan that looks like everybody else's—which means **their young children are an afterthought, not the center of their plan.**

I have a client who is very successful financially. He is divorced and has two young children under age ten. His estate plan had been set up years ago by a very reputable and expensive law firm in Orange County, California. The problem was that the estate plan they set up for him disproportionately focused on tax avoidance, with little consideration for how those tax avoidance strategies would impact his children.

Yes, they ensured that there would be a lot of money going to his children because taxes would be significantly reduced, but there was little emphasis on the best way to pass the money to the children and how that would impact the children developing their independence and self-reliance. In other words, they set his kids up to be "trust fund babies": kids with unlimited wealth at a young age, no restrictions, no protections, and no incentive to become their own people.

When I asked him why he chose to pass his money to his children this way, he asked, *Did I have a choice? They didn't tell me there was another option.* I was floored. My friend paid over $30,000 for his estate plan, and what he got would never work for his family the way he intended. That is because his children were not the center of his estate plan.

The hourly bill. The big law firms usually bill their clients by the hour, which means the client doesn't know beforehand what the final bill will be. The reason they bill by the hour, instead of a flat rate, is because their whole business model and revenue is based upon attorneys billing a set numbers of hours every year.

The attorneys subconsciously know they need to make their billable hours or get fired. This leaves them with two masters to serve: you and the billable clock. The more they bill you, the closer they get to their quota. Even if they don't want to bill you for every time you call or e-mail them, they *have* to; if they don't bill for the time they interact with you, they won't meet their quota or they'll have to make up for it outside of normal hours.

The billable hour is terrible for attorneys (most of them hate it), but it's even worse for the client since it prevents them from making an educated decision beforehand about whether the service they are paying for will be worth the cost. It also prevents clients from being able to budget. Most of all, **the hourly bill structure makes clients afraid to talk to the attorney because they don't want to have a huge bill!**

The one-size-fits-all documents. Big law firms typically have their own standard form templates that they've always used. When they get a new client, they add in the relevant names and make a few changes. This is a very common yet dangerous way to practice law. I can't tell you how many times people come into my office with the estate plan they had prepared elsewhere, and when I go through it with them and ask why they chose to pass money a certain way to someone, they look at me and say, "We never knew we had a choice." I also am very troubled at how many estate plans have the wrong names or missing sentences, a clear sign that the attorney used copy and paste to turn an old client's estate plan into a new one for someone else.

Goodbye, so long, it was nice to have met you. The big law firms are designed to help someone get an estate plan and then send them on their way. There really is no expectation or service for a continued relationship with the client after they get a plan in place.

The problem with this is that an estate plan is only good if it works at the time it needs to work, not the day you get it. If you don't have an ongoing relationship with your attorney, then how can you make sure your estate plan keeps up with your changing needs?

It's very likely that the home you currently live in or the people you choose today to serve as your guardians is going to be different when you pass away. You need a lifelong relationship with your attorney to ensure that your plan is continually updated, and they need to have a system that ensures continual contact with you. You also want an attorney your family can turn to if the unthinkable really does happen.

What about Small Firms?

I like the idea of a small firm because it seems so much more personable. Unfortunately, most small firm lawyers are practicing law the same way they did at the big firm. They may discount their rates since they tend to not have the fancy overhead, but the tradeoff is that most lack the infrastructure that the big law firms have to help consistently process the clients.

At the big law firm, we always knew when someone was about to quit. They would download all the documents they could and get ready to run. How many lawyers use these forms on their next clients, but never update them? Many small firms don't have the revenue or resources to keep their documents updated when the laws change.

While your small firm lawyer will probably be a really nice guy, he just won't be able to provide you the high level of service you will need throughout your lifetime. If your attorney runs a one-person firm and practices a lot of other areas of law in addition to estate planning, or is also the notary, the receptionist, the secretary, the janitor, and the file clerk, then that's a very clear sign that the firm cannot provide your family with the ongoing support needed for an effective estate plan.

Oftentimes, you are better off saving yourself the money and trying to do your planning yourself online, because you are really not getting any greater of a benefit by using this type of attorney than you would by just going online.

Option Two: Do It Yourself Online

Online legal systems seem like a great solution for those of us who don't want to be dragged into an attorney's office and pay high hourly rates just to get boilerplate templates that look very similar to the ones you can cheaply buy online. And with all of the costs we have when raising a young family, who wouldn't want to save a few dollars?

Unfortunately, **working with online legal systems is even more dangerous than using a big law firm or a small firm lawyer.** Still, due to great marketing, many people are convinced that these types of services will work.

Remember that story I told you earlier about how I downloaded a will and slapped my name on it? That is the equivalent of people trying to go online and thinking everything is taken care of. It just doesn't work.

I was at a dinner party a few years ago in Sonoma, California, and a very wealthy, well-known physician, boldly asked me what the difference was between me and online legal sites. I smiled and said, "I don't know, what's the difference between you and WebMD.com?"

Obviously, there is huge difference between attempting to do your estate planning yourselves versus hiring a reputable lawyer to help you. **I believe that the main reason people try to do their estate planning themselves is because they are misled into believing that knowing *about* something translates into knowing how to *do* something.**

Information is so readily available online that people often blur the line between getting educated and getting properly trained. The truth is:

Reading Dr. Phil books does not make us therapists;

Watching HGTV does not make us home builders;

Listening to Dr. Oz does not make us surgeons;

Seeing P90X infomercials does not make us fit;

And reading estate planning books or websites does not make us estate planning attorneys.

You don't need to take my biased word for it either. Online legal planning systems have warnings and disclaimers all over them telling you they do not give legal advice and to consult with an attorney before you download their boilerplate forms.

The other problem you face is that online systems aren't accountable to you for the plan you created through them, and they do not have a fiduciary duty to your family. There is no objective third party to carefully guide you when you make important decisions affecting your loved ones. And in your family's time of crisis there is no one to turn to who knows you and clearly understands your wishes.

If you lost your spouse tomorrow, do you think you could call up an online legal site and ask them to help you? No! You'd be stuck at ground zero googling local estate planning attorneys who never knew you or your spouse and had not been part of the "estate plan" you've already locked yourself into.

Remember that saying that if something it too good to be true, it probably is? That's Internet legal docs for you.

Make sure that you create your plan with a trusted estate planning attorney who regularly guides families with young children!

How to Evaluate an Estate Planning Attorney

We've talked about the dangers of working with traditional estate planning law firms and using online systems if you are going to create a plan that protects your kids and helps them if the unthinkable happens. By now you are probably wondering, *who can help me with my planning?* Believe me, I can relate! When my husband and I saw all of the gaps with traditional law firms and online planning when it came to protecting our own kids, we also felt option-less. That was a major motivation for us to dedicate our law practice to helping other families with young children.

Over the past several years, Meier Law Firm has helped hundreds of families with young children set up comprehensive estate plans that center around their children. We have the infrastructure, resources, and integrity to serve our families for their lifetimes, and that for us is mission accomplished!

By using the Attorney Checklist below, you can have the same confidence in your attorney as our clients have in us. Before you hire any prospective attorney or law firm, be 100% sure they can provide your family the full protection and services you need.

The Attorney Checklist

1. Is the firm created for the primary purpose of helping parents with young children set up estate plans that protect the entire family?

2. Does the firm build custom estate plans for each client using the best technology and resources, rather than cramming clients into a one-size-fits-all template document that does not account for a family's specific needs?

3. Do they offer a mini estate plan for children that protects children from temporary foster care and court, and ensures that their emergency medical decisions can be made by people their parents have chosen?

4. Do they follow a set process so each client has a consistent, exceptional experience and will receive their completed estate plan by a designated date?

5. Do they regularly guide and coach families with young children, and have proven techniques and processes to ensure you will make the best-educated decisions for your children's security?

6. Do they build safeguards into their estate plans that protect you during the "gap period" (the time from the moment something happens to you until the time someone administers your estate plan)?

7. Do they provide you options for protecting money you leave behind so your spouse and children could never lose it to a future divorce, creditors, lawsuits, bankruptcy, or ill-intentioned third parties?

8. Does the firm work on a flat-fee basis so you can ask questions and make an educated decision on the services provided without accumulating an hourly bill?

9. Do they offer you a lifelong relationship as your trusted advisor who can help keep your estate plan current with life's changes and the law?

10. Will they provide free reviews of your estate plan?

11. Will the firm help you preserve your memories, dreams, and values, so your loved ones will always know how much you love them and what you want for them?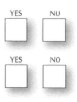

12. Do you trust the firm to be there for your family in their time of need?

If your prospective attorney can check every "YES" box—hire them! You'll be getting the essential protections your family needs. But if they can't check all the "YES" boxes, they are probably not the best firm for you. I cannot think of one criterion on the Attorney Checklist that can be eliminated without jeopardizing your kids' protection. To get connected with a family trust attorney who regularly works with families with young children, we invite you to contact Meier Law Firm today. If we cannot help, we can connect you with an attorney who can. Let me encourage you to start your planning today.

If your prospective attorney can check every "YES" box—hire them! You'll be getting the essential protections your family needs.

But if they can't check all the "YES" boxes, they are probably not the best firm for you. I cannot think of one criterion on the Attorney Checklist that can be eliminated without jeopardizing your kids' protection.

To get connected with a family trust attorney who regularly works with families with young children, we invite you to contact Meier Law Firm today. If we cannot help, we can connect you with an attorney who can. Let me encourage you to start your planning today.

Additional Resources for Your Family from Meier Law Firm

1. **Attend an Achieve Your Dreams Planning Session**

   Want to get personalized advice on what type of estate plan your family may need? If you live in or own property in California, we invite you to schedule an Achieve Your Dreams Planning Session with Meier Law Firm. Sessions can be conducted virtually or at our offices in Newport Beach, California. Visit meierfirm.com today or call 949.718.0420 to learn more.

2. **Attend a Kids Guardian Workshop**

   Join us at our popular Kids Guardian Workshop, where a Meier Law Firm attorney will help you name permanent guardians for your kids. Visit meierevents.com or call 949.718.0420 to find an upcoming Kids Guardian Workshop near you.

3. **Get our Prosperous Family Weekly Email**

   Keep in touch with Josh and Laura Meier and receive our weekly quick-step for becoming a prosperous family. Our Prosperous Family Weekly Email is fun, fast, and educational, and is sure to make a positive difference to your week!

4. **Follow Meier Law Firm Online**

    Follow us online and receive important tips, offers, and alerts that are essential to your family's well-being.

    Facebook: www.facebook.com/meierfirm

    Instagram: www.instagram.com/meierlawfirm

    Linkedin: www.linkedin.com/in/lmeier

    Twitter: www.twitter.com/LKMeier